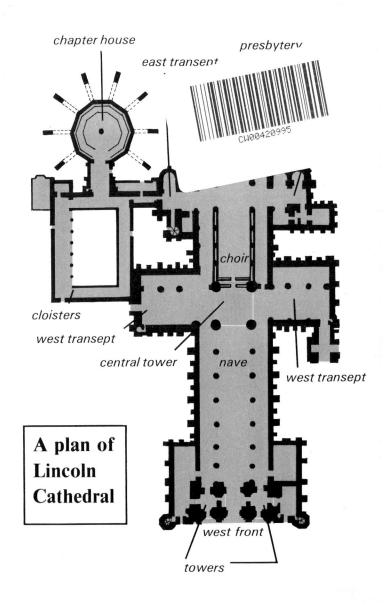

chapter house

presbytery

east transept

CW00420995

choir

cloisters

west transept

central tower

nave

west transept

A plan of Lincoln Cathedral

west front

towers

CONTENTS

Cover: York Minster   *Back cover:* Roof of Ely Cathedral
Title page: Ely Cathedral

Acknowledgments
The illustrations on the front endpaper and pages 5, 6, 10, 14, 16, 20, 25, 38, 43 and 52 are by Gavin Rowe.
Photographs on pages 12, 14 (bottom), 20, 24 (top), 30, 34, 46/47 and 51 are by Aerofilms Limited; those on pages 44 and 45 are by J. A. Joy; and the photographs on the cover, title page and back cover, also pages 4, 5, 6, 7, 8, 9, 10 (2), 11 (2), 13, 14 (top), 15, 16, 17, 18, 19 (3), 21, 22/23, 23, 24 (bottom), 25 (top), 26, 27 (2), 28 (2), 29, 31, 32/33, 33, 35 (2), 36 (2), 37 (3), 38 (top), 39, 40 (2), 41 (2), 42, 43 (top), 48, 49 (2) and 50 are by Woodmansterne.
Designed by Graham Marlow.

British Library Cataloguing in Publication Data

Seward, Anthony
  Cathedrals.
    1. Great Britain. Cathedrals, to 1985 –
  For children
  I. Title
  941

    ISBN 0-7214-1092-8

First edition

Published by Ladybird Books Ltd Loughborough Leicestershire UK
Ladybird Books Inc Auburn Maine 04210 USA

Printed in England

DISCOVERING
Cathedrals

by ANTHONY SEWARD BA

Ladybird Books

Canterbury Cathedral

One event is outstanding in Canterbury's history – the terrible murder of Thomas Becket, the Archbishop, in the cathedral on 29th December 1170. His skull was split open by two knights who thought they were carrying out the orders of their King, Henry II. Becket was made a saint only two years later, and his shrine quickly became one of the three most popular in Europe. Pilgrims came in their thousands to pay homage and to seek miracle cures.

They were overawed by the richness of the shrine, with its gold and jewels, and its setting. As they knelt to pray, they must have been dazzled not only by the light from hundreds of candles, but also by the light from the windows of the Corona ('Becket's Crown').

Crypt under Canterbury Cathedral choir

The magnificent shrine was destroyed at the Reformation in 1538 and Becket's body now lies in a simple tomb.

The cathedral was founded by St Augustine on his mission to England in 597, and it houses the throne of the Archbishop of Canterbury, head of the Anglican Church.

The present building owes most to four men: Archbishop Lanfranc, who started it in 1070; William of Sens and his successor William the Englishman, who continued the Norman part of the work; and Henry Yevele, who redesigned the nave in the Perpendicular style in 1374. The fine central tower known as 'Bell Harry' was added about the year 1495.

A detail from the Thomas Becket window

5

St Paul's Cathedral

For nearly three centuries, St Paul's Cathedral has been the noble setting for Britain's most solemn state occasions, from royal weddings to the funerals of famous leaders such as Nelson and Churchill.

St Paul's is the only major English cathedral to have been built all at one time – between 1675 and 1710 – to the design of a single architect. When the Great Fire of London destroyed the old medieval cathedral in 1666, Sir Christopher Wren was given a free hand to design his masterpiece, and the finest craftsmen in the country to build it.

The cathedral's most famous feature, the dome, is quite separate from the dome you can see from inside. In between the two there is space for a strong cone of brick, and it is this, and not the outer dome of lead, which really supports the gilded cross, 111.3 m (365 ft) from the ground.

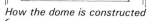

outer dome

brick cone

inner dome

How the dome is constructed

The choir and high altar of St Paul's

6

Westminster Cathedral

Westminster Cathedral, built between 1895 and 1903, is the chief Roman Catholic church in England.

The first design for it, in the Early English style, was rejected as being too like nearby Westminster Abbey.

Instead the architect, J F Bentley, created a Byzantine building more like some of the churches in Italy, Greece and Turkey. The bands of brick and stone on the tall campanile (bell tower) are similar to those on Siena Cathedral, and the domes are like those on St Mark's, Venice, and those on St Sophia, Constantinople. Inside, over one hundred kinds of marble cover the walls and arches, and there are rich mosaics on the ceiling, giving a splendid effect.

St Paul's Chapel, Westminster Cathedral

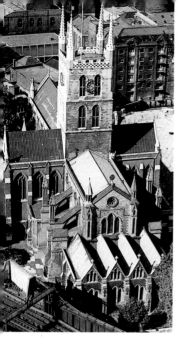

Southwark Cathedral

No cathedral in England is closer to the bustle of city life. It is at the south end of London Bridge, next to a railway viaduct, and is surrounded by offices, shops and warehouses. Until the Reformation, Southwark Cathedral was attached to the priory of St Mary Overie (meaning 'over the river'). It became a parish church, but by 1890 was almost a ruin. Fortunately, Southwark then became a bishopric and the old church was restored and rebuilt, in time for its first bishop's enthronement in 1905.

Look for the colourful effigy of John Gower the poet (who died in 1408) with his head pillowed on his three major books. Also worth seeing is the superb 1690 candelabrum made of brass and wrought iron – one of the finest in Britain.

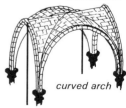

This shows how the vaulting in the retrochoir is constructed

curved arch

pointed arch

Retrochoir, Southwark Cathedral

St Alban's Cathedral

St Alban was a Roman soldier who became the first Christian martyr in Britain. Because he had sheltered a priest, he was beheaded, on the hill where the cathedral now stands. The shrine set up on the spot soon became a popular place of pilgrimage.

Parts of the cathedral date from 1077, and the nave is the second longest in England (after Winchester), at 153 m (550 ft). The Norman tower is an interesting link with Verulamium (Roman St Alban's), since it was built of red bricks taken from the old city. There are some well preserved medieval wall paintings to see, and a richly carved fifteenth century rood screen.

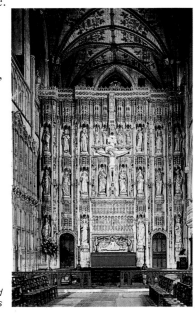

High altar and reredos, St Alban's

From the air

Ely Cathedral

Twenty five and a half kilometres (sixteen miles) north
of Cambridge is the small market town of Ely, built on
a rise surrounded by fenland. Before the fens were
drained in the seventeenth century, the Isle of Ely was a
real island, surrounded by marshes.

You can see the huge cathedral from quite a long way
away, looming like a great ship over the flat countryside.
Although remote from any big cities, it is one of the
noblest of English cathedrals, with a magnificent
Norman nave. It was started in 1083.

The cathedral's chief glory, however, is the Octagon, an
eight sided tower topped by a wooden lantern. It was

built by Alan de Walsingham to replace the central tower which collapsed in 1322, and is a masterpiece of engineering skill. The main purpose of the lantern is to let extra light into the nave. It is supported by eight massive oak timbers, each 19.2 m (63 ft) long by 0.9 m (3 ft) square – the whole of England had to be searched for trees big enough to supply them.

Along one side of the cathedral close is the King's School, founded by Henry VIII. Like its namesake at Canterbury, it provides boy singers for the choir. This part of the country is well known for choral music. Besides Ely there are the world famous King's College and St John's College choirs in Cambridge – all three in friendly rivalry with each other.

Detail of roof

Norwich Cathedral

Norwich Cathedral has three striking features. They are the tower – the tallest and one of the most graceful Norman towers in England – the spire, and the flying buttresses supporting the eastern end. This form of buttress

flying buttress

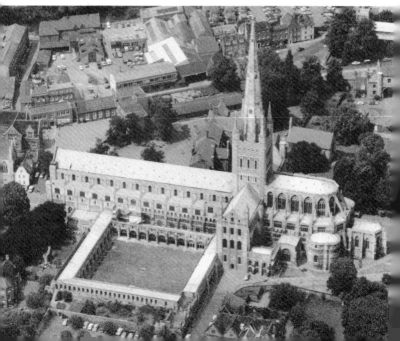

was invented to support the upper part of tall buildings, and often gives a light and airy effect as it 'flies' across space.

The nave is unusual in that its lower arches are the same height as the upper arches in the triforium. They are Norman, but the roof is a superb lierne vault added in the fifteenth century (*lierne* means that the main ribs

Choir vault, Norwich Cathedral

supporting the vault are linked to each other by other ribs, creating a network). About a third of the way along the vault you will notice a hole, as if one of the roof bosses were missing. Through this the monks used to lower a swinging container of burning incense at Pentecost, in memory of the day when the Holy Ghost descended on the Apostles in tongues of flame.

Cathedrals are named after the *cathedra* or bishop's throne that each one contains as the mother church of its diocese. The throne at Norwich is the oldest still used in England, and dates back to the eighth century.

Peterborough Cathedral

The splendours of Peterborough begin with its West Front – three lofty arches 24.7 m (81 ft) high, with a turret on each side. In the centre arch is a rather odd-looking porch probably added at a later date to give extra support after a weakness had been found.

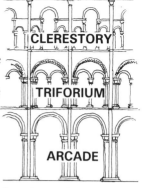

The West Front is Early English, but the main part of the cathedral is pure Norman. The beautiful nave has arches at three levels: arcade, triforium and clerestory. Its wooden roof was painted in 1220 in a pattern of diamonds containing pictures of kings, saints, bishops and monsters. Instead of craning your neck to look at it, though, you may view it in comfort by using the mobile mirror provided!

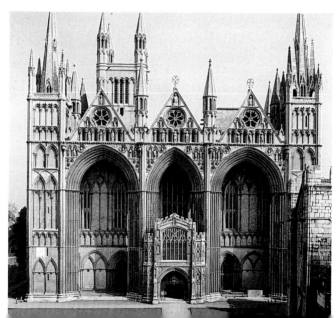

The rounded Norman arches of the chancel

Two famous queens were buried here – Mary Queen of
Scots and Catherine of Aragon, first wife of Henry VIII.
Mary's body was removed twenty five years later to
Westminster Abbey by her son James I, but you can
find Catherine's tomb in the chancel. Both were buried
by the old gravedigger Robert Scarlett, whose portrait is
just inside the west door.

Southwell Minster

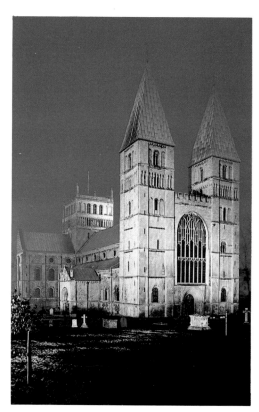

Southwell is famous for its wealth of delicate stone carvings – of trees, flowers, animals and people. You could spend hours in the chapter house alone, admiring the skilled work of the thirteenth century craftsmen on the entrance arch and interior. Leaves of trees and plants such as oaks, vines and hops are shown in exact living detail. Often they share the scene with animals or men – a huntsman sounding his horn under a tree, a goat eating ivy leaves, pigs rooting up acorns.

And if you would like to know what ordinary people in the Middle Ages looked like, go to the choir screen. Here the carvers included portraits of many of their fellow workmen, looking just as they did in everyday life – one scratching his leg, another tugging his beard. In the choir itself, again there are numerous carvings of leaves and fruits, especially in the small square panels lining the back of the bishop's throne. Every one of these shows a different kind of foliage.

The brass eagle lectern in the choir once belonged to the monks at nearby Newstead Abbey. When the monasteries were closed down, they threw it into a lake to save it from Henry VIII's men. Then, in 1805, it was rediscovered in a Nottingham shop and presented to Southwell.

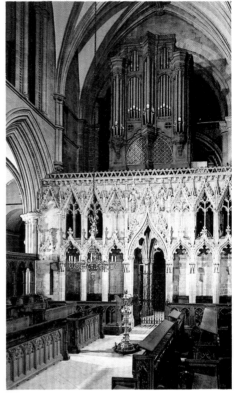

Choir screen and organ

Archbishop Sandys' tomb

Carved capital in the chapter house: pigs eating acorns

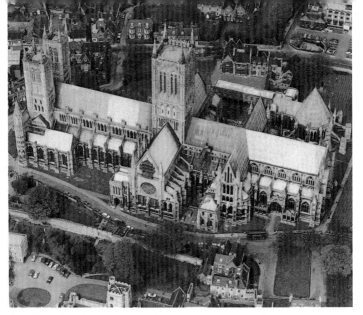

From the air

Lincoln Cathedral

Lincoln Cathedral stands on top of a steep hill, its setting rivalled only by that of Durham. It feels more like part of a medieval city than most other English cathedrals do. The best view of it is from the Castle, across a square, and you go to it through ancient houses and shops, and the fourteenth century Exchequer Gate.

The West Front

Parts of the West Front are Norman and carry curious sculptures of Daniel in the lions' den, Noah's Ark, and other scenes. Most of the cathedral, however, was rebuilt after a violent earthquake in 1185. It was largely finished by 1380 and is, like Salisbury, built entirely in the Early English style, with no later additions.

The chapter house

The two windows known as the Bishop's Eye and the Dean's Eye face each other at either end of the transept. They are outstanding for their flowing tracery (ornamental work) and the Dean's eye still has its original thirteenth century glass, an even rarer treasure.

Behind the main choir is the Angel Choir, named after the angels carved between the arches of the triforium. Here may be seen the famous Lincoln Imp, but someone will have to tell you how to find him!

York Minster

St Augustine sent missionaries to convert England in 597. He intended the new Church to be ruled from the former Roman capitals of London and York. London never got its Archbishop, but St Paulinus was appointed at York in about 672, and the English Church in Northern England has been governed from there ever since.

Several earlier churches stood on the site of York Minster, but the present building was begun by Archbishop Walter de Gray in 1220. It took two hundred and fifty years to complete and contains superb work in every style of the period, from Early English to Perpendicular. The largest Gothic church in England, it is also admired as one of the finest in all Europe.

The most outstanding of all the beauties of York is its wealth of stained glass. There are over one hundred windows, and the surviving medieval glass alone would cover over a fifth of a hectare (0.5 acre). Look especially for the graceful Five Sisters window and for St Catherine's rose window, featuring the white rose of York and the red rose of Lancaster.

The chapter house is notable for having no central pillar to support the vaulted roof. Above it is a room used by the medieval masons which still shows some of their working patterns scratched on the floor.

York underwent major restoration in the 1960s, when thousands of tonnes of concrete were poured in to secure the foundations. The original supports had been nothing more than wooden piles, which had rotted away over the centuries.

Rose window, south transept

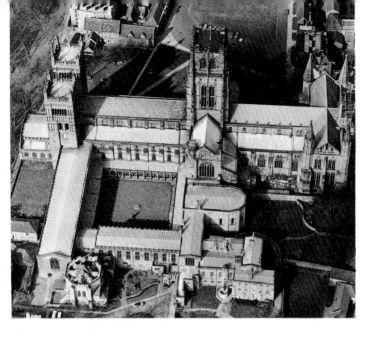

Durham Cathedral

No British cathedral has a grander site than Durham's. Standing high on a cliff overlooking the River Wear, it had been a favourite subject of artists and photographers for centuries.

When the Norsemen in 876 sacked Lindisfarne Abbey on Holy Island, off the coast of Northumberland, the monks fled to the mainland. With them they

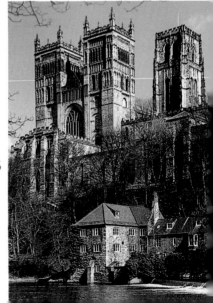

took the body of St Cuthbert, who had been Bishop of Lindisfarne two hundred years earlier. But it was not until 999, after much wandering, that his remains finally came to rest at Durham, where a small cathedral was built over his tomb.

The present building was started in 1093, following the Norman Conquest. Bishop William de Carileph had been banished to the North for three years by King William Rufus for taking part in a rebellion.

Organ and choir stalls, Durham Cathedral

However, he had always wanted to build a church to rival the great cathedrals of Northern France, and this gave him his chance. Although there have been many later additions, Durham Cathedral is still overwhelmingly Norman. This is especially so inside where the most striking feature is the range of massive round columns carved with zigzag and diamond patterns.

On the northwest door there is a sanctuary knocker. Anyone fleeing from justice who could clasp its ring would be given shelter by the monks for up to thirty seven days.

Arches in Galilee chapel

St Mary's Cathedral, Edinburgh

During Queen Victoria's reign there was a great revival
of medieval styles in church building. In the 1870s
Sir George Gilbert Scott, who had spent many years
restoring medieval churches, won a competition to
design a large cathedral in Edinburgh. This had been
made possible by a gift of land from two sisters,
Barbara and Mary Walker. Scott admired the Early
English style above all and tried to put its best features
into what became his finest building, the Cathedral
Church of St Mary's.

The cathedral has three spires, like Lichfield, but here
they are much higher and more impressive. The building
can be seen from many parts of the city, and stands out
clearly in most views of the famous Edinburgh skyline.

St Giles, Edinburgh

The High Church of St Giles, often known as St Giles' Cathedral, stands near the top of Edinburgh's Royal Mile, which runs down a steep hill from the castle on its rock to the Palace of Holyroodhouse. Because of St Giles' high position, its central tower, topped with a crown-shaped lantern, can be seen from most parts of the city. It was built mainly in the fourteenth and fifteenth centuries, but heavily restored in the nineteenth, so that much of the stonework you now see dates from that time. However, one of its most impressive features is the chapel of the Most Ancient and Most Noble Order of the Thistle, built in 1911 to a design by Sir Robert Lorimer and displaying the colourful stalls and banners of the knights. The Order of the Thistle is Scotland's highest order of chivalry, as the Order of the Garter is England's. St Giles has witnessed many of the great events of Scottish history, and has had many changes of fortune – at different times it has served as a court, shops, a prison and police station, as well as being divided at one period into three churches.

Knights' crests, Thistle Chapel

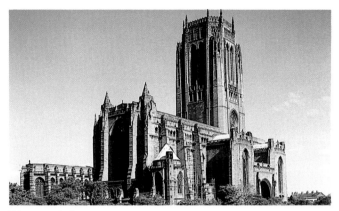

Liverpool Cathedral

The sheer size of Liverpool's Anglican Cathedral is awe inspiring – only St Peter's in Rome is bigger. Everything about it is huge, from the cliff-like walls to the massive bells, the heaviest in the world. It is the only Gothic cathedral to have been built since the Reformation and rivals the great medieval churches in its detailed craftsmanship.

Like the medieval cathedrals, it took a long time to build. It was started in 1904, by the architect Giles Gilbert Scott who was only twenty two when he won the competition to design it. (He was the grandson of the man who designed St Mary's, Edinburgh.) When he died in 1960 it was still unfinished, but the great building was finally completed in 1978.

The organ, Liverpool Cathedral

The Metropolitan Cathedral, Liverpool

The full name of Liverpool's Roman Catholic Cathedral is the Metropolitan Cathedral of Christ the King. It is the newest in Britain, built entirely in the 1960s to a design by Sir Frederick Gibberd. It is circular in shape and rises up to a spiky crown, looking down on the city from a high hill.

Inside is an immense open space filled with blue light from the windows, with the glowing crown high above. The altar is in the centre so that everyone in the congregation can take part equally in the services.

Beside the cathedral there is a large concrete space. This covers the crypt, all that was built of an earlier design by Sir Edwin Lutyens. His cathedral would have had a dome larger than St Peter's in Rome, but it had to be abandoned as too expensive.

Chester Cathedral

Before the Reformation in the sixteenth century, Chester had been an abbey. Henry VIII raised it to cathedral rank, and the abbot became the first dean (responsible, with the canons, for running the cathedral).

The fourteenth century church was heavily restored by the Victorians. The domestic buildings used by the monks however have remained almost unchanged, so that you can see what monastic life was like. As well as

Chester Cathedral from the air

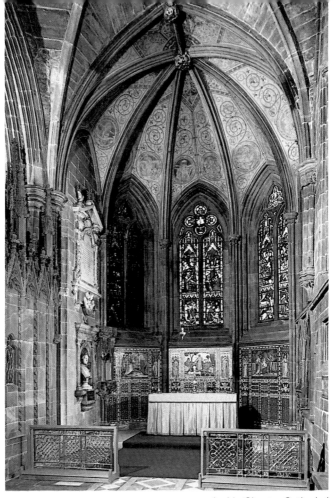

Inside Chester Cathedral

the cloisters and chapter house, where the business
meetings of the community were held, there is the large
refectory, or dining hall. In the hall is a handsome stone
pulpit for readings during meals, reached by an unusual
stairway built into the wall behind it.

Coventry Cathedral

The medieval cathedral was destroyed by fire in the worst air raid suffered by any English city during the Second World War. But the outer walls, tower and spire were left standing, and they have been preserved as a reminder of the waste of war. Where the old altar stood there is now a cross made of charred timbers from the old church. Carved on the wall behind it are the simple words 'Father, Forgive.'

The new cathedral, designed by Sir Basil Spence and completed in 1962, is linked to the old by a covered porch. A vast clear glass window at the back of the building means that you can always see the ruins from inside the main part of the cathedral.

Baptistry window

Graham Sutherland's huge tapestry of Christ in Glory, with the little figure of Man between his feet, dominates the interior. It is thought to be the largest tapestry in the world and took thirty thousand hours to weave.

Some of Britain's best modern artists contributed to Coventry Cathedral. John Piper designed the Baptistry window, a blaze of colour and light symbolising the power of the Holy Spirit in the world. There is a chunky bronze eagle by Elizabeth Frink on the lectern. Most dramatic of all is Sir Jacob Epstein's sculpture of St Michael defeating the Devil, on the outside wall facing the road.

From the air

Lichfield Cathedral

Lichfield is the only English medieval cathedral that still has three spires – they are known as 'the Ladies of the Vale'. It suffered badly from the Parliamentary troops in the Civil War. They shot away the central spire, took the lead from the roofs, and smashed images and stained glass. It took two centuries to repair the damage.

The cathedral was built mostly between 1195 and 1325 to house the popular shrine of St Chad, bishop of Mercia in the seventh century. When Mercia was the most powerful Saxon kingdom under King Offa, for a while Lichfield even had its own archbishop.

Look for the lovely sculpture of sleeping figures by Sir Francis Chantrey. It is a monument to two children who died in 1812.

The chapter house

The ''Sleeping Children'' monument

Worcester Cathedral

One of the most photographed views in England is that
of Worcester Cathedral – either from the opposite bank
of the River Severn or from the county cricket ground.
It is easy to see why.

Worcester Cathedral   The sanctuary

The cathedral grew over a long period and shows good
examples of each building style, from early Norman to
Tudor, as well as a great deal of Victorian restoration. It
contains the earliest royal effigy, on the tomb of King
John who died in 1216. Look out also for the fine
chantry chapel where the body of Prince Arthur lies. He
was the eldest son of Henry VII, and he died in 1502 at
the age of fifteen.

Hereford Cathedral

Although the cathedral is medieval, it was clumsily restored in the eighteenth and nineteenth centuries and you have to look carefully to find the original parts. The best feature is the central tower, completed in the fourteenth century.

Hereford's most famous treasure is a map of the world, painted in about 1275. It measures 1.65 m by 1.35 m (65 in by 53 in) and shows all that was believed at the time about the world. Jerusalem is at the centre, with East at the top and Britain in the bottom left hand corner. Each area is shown with its own animals, some real, some fabulous, such as men with dogs' heads.

The 13th century Mappa Mundi

The chained library

Gloucester Cathedral

In 1327 Edward II was brutally murdered in a dungeon at Berkeley Castle. Fearing his powerful enemies, the churches at Bristol and Malmesbury refused to accept the body for burial. It finally came to rest at Gloucester, in a handsome tomb carrying an alabaster effigy of the king.

His son Edward III encouraged people to believe in his father as

a saintly martyr. The tomb became a popular place of pilgrimage, bringing in money for the church. Because of this, the monks were able to remodel the Norman cathedral in the new Perpendicular style, twenty years before it was used anywhere else. Gloucester is thus the birthplace of Perpendicular, which is only found in England. As at Winchester, the change was made not by rebuilding, but by encasing the Norman pillars and arches in newly carved stonework.

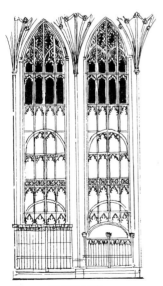

Perpendicular style

The cloister has the earliest fan vaulting in the country. Other interesting features which have survived there include the monks' *lavatorium* (washing place) and *carrels* (tiny cells used as studies). In this warm and sheltered place, it is easy to imagine the monks reading or at work patiently illuminating (painting and gilding) the letters of a great Bible or prayer book.

Quire and east window, Gloucester Cathedral

Llandaff Cathedral, Cardiff

The present cathedral arose from the ruins of earlier buildings. After being nearly destroyed three times, most recently by a landmine in the Second World War, it was completely restored in 1960. Luckily it was possible to keep many

The nave, looking east

of the old parts, some dating back to the twelfth century.

Inside is a fitting symbol of the cathedral's survival against such odds – Sir Jacob Epstein's great aluminium statue of Christ in Majesty. It is

Llandaff Cathedral

mounted on a hollow
cylinder containing
the organ, itself
supported by huge
concrete arches over
the nave. The slits
around it are openings
for the organ pipes,
appearing between
gilded saints and
angels saved from the
old choirstalls.

The font

*A painting by
Rossetti called
"The Seed of David"*

Wells Cathedral

Wells is one of the smaller cathedrals, but it is one of the most beautiful. It lies in a peaceful rural setting by the bishop's palace and moat, where swans ring a bell to be fed.

It is best known for its magnificent West Front, a stone screen which contains over three hundred statues. But the most unusual feature is inside. Under the central tower are three

scissors arch

arches which are mirrored by arches built upside down above them – rather like pairs of stone scissors. The effect is both strong and graceful, an inspired solution to a serious problem – they were in fact built to strengthen the tower, which had begun to tilt dangerously by 1338, only twenty years after it was built.

Wells has two other treasures that you shouldn't miss. One is its extraordinary astronomical clock. As each hour strikes, four knights on horseback come out. Then they joust, and one is unseated. And look for the amusing series of carved capitals on the columns. One set of four tells the complete story of some apple stealers raiding an orchard, and how they were caught!

Truro Cathedral

Cornwall only became a separate diocese in 1876 (previously it had been part of the diocese of Exeter).

The cathedral was designed by J L Pearson in the Early English style and built between 1880 and 1910. The three main towers are all crowned with spires, so that the building looks as if it is soaring up from its rather cramped site.

Inside Truro Cathedral

Pearson included part of the sixteenth century parish church in his design, and the monuments from the older church were also kept. See if you can find the slate headstone to Owen Phippen, who died in 1636, and read its account of his adventures in Turkey. It is by the south window of St Mary's aisle.

Exeter Cathedral

The West Front, like that at Wells, has a fine array of statues. They are mainly of kings of England and saints, and date from 1350 onwards like most of the cathedral.

Once you are inside the building, the sight is breathtaking. The longest unbroken line of medieval vaulting in the world stretches for 91.5 m (300 ft) into the distance. From the pillars of the nave spring clusters of stone ribs, like a grove of palm trees. These meet in a series of stone roof bosses along the centre of the vault. The purpose of the bosses is to cover the joints of the ribs, but they are works of art in themselves, because each one is richly carved and coloured. Some show whole scenes such as the Crucifixion or the murder of Becket. Others show musicians, or heads of people who were known to the carvers, and still others show foliage and flowers.

The misericords placed under choir seats in many great churches are always interesting. Those at Exeter are famous for their variety, quality and age. They are probably the oldest in England, dating from the thirteenth century, and include an elephant and a mermaid.

Overlooking the nave, opposite the north porch, is an unusual stone minstrels' gallery. Fourteen angels stand in the niches, playing musical instruments which include bagpipes, a recorder, a trumpet, and cymbals.

Exeter Cathedral from the air

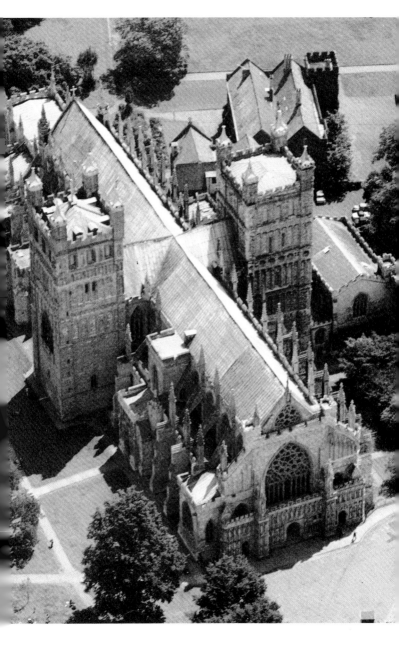

Salisbury Cathedral

The city of Salisbury was founded in 1220, when the people of Old Sarum migrated from their barren hilltop to the fertile valley below. Building of the cathedral began immediately and was finished in only sixty years (most English medieval cathedrals took several centuries to build). So it is an almost perfect example of the style of one period – Early English.

The famous spire was not part of the original design. There was always a tower of course, but the spire was not added until 1334. It is the highest in England, at

123.2 m (404 ft), and is supported inside by a complicated arrangement of wooden timbers. The stonework had to be as light as possible for the tower to carry it, and it is only 23 cm (9 in) thick. Part of the interest and beauty of the spire comes from the three bands of stone tracery on it, which repeat patterns

Choir and sanctuary, Salisbury Cathedral

from the tower below. Inside the cathedral, the careful patterning continues. The windows and arches echo each other at each level, their outline emphasised by slender columns of dark polished Purbeck stone. The overall effect is cool, dignified and harmonious.

The Mompesson tomb

49

Winchester Cathedral

Set in the ancient Saxon capital of Wessex and England, Winchester Cathedral reflects the royal history of the city. Several of the Saxon kings, and Canute and his wife Emma, are buried here. So is William Rufus. Here too Mary Tudor was married to Philip of Spain – the chair she sat in during the ceremony can still be seen.

After the Norman Conquest, Bishop Walkelin began the present building, in 1079. It is the longest Gothic church in Europe, at 169.6 m (536 ft). The Norman part of the cathedral survives unchanged in the north and south transepts, but most of the rest is later. The nave was transformed by William of Wykeham (Bishop from 1367 to 1404) into a fine example of the Perpendicular style. Its lofty columns and intricate fan vaulting give a great impression of height. Rather than rebuilding completely, his masons encased the original Norman columns in stone shaped to fit the new style.

Baptismal font

The unusual font is of black Tournai marble carved with scenes from the life of St Nicholas. Other features to look out for are the memorials to the novelist Jane Austen and the great fisherman Izaak Walton, the misericords under the choir seats, and the shrine of St Swithin,

Winchester Cathedral from the air

an early Bishop of Winchester who died in 862. The story goes that he asked to be buried outside his cathedral. Then, when his remains were later transferred to the *inside*, it rained for forty days. This is why some people nowadays believe that a rainy St Swithin's Day – 15th July – means that a similar spell of wet weather will follow.

Glossary

arcade
A row of arches

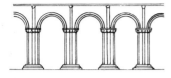

(*see also* Peterborough)

boss
A carved piece of wood or stone covering a point where vault ribs meet

clerestory
Upper windows letting light in over an aisle
(*see* Peterborough)

fan vaulting
Type of vault invented in the fourteenth century

flying buttress
A support crossing a space
(*see* Norwich)

lantern
A tower with windows above the surrounding roofs (*see* Ely)

lectern
A reading stand

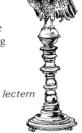

lectern

misericord
A ledge on a tip-up seat in a choirstall, often with carving underneath. This one shows footballers in the Middle Ages

rood/choir screen
Screen separating the choir from the rest of the church, sometimes carrying a large crucifix, or 'rood'

triforium
A gallery, usually above an arcade and below a clerestory
(*see* Peterborough)

Reformation
The fifteenth century religious movement which brought Reformed or Protestant churches into being